CW00689942

Living Lord

Lesley Husselbee & Simon Oxley

NATIONAL CHRISTIAN EDUCATION COUNCIL

Other worship resources published by NCEC

Celebrating Series . . .

A series of six books for all-age festival services:
Celebrating Christmas Books 1 & 2
Celebrating Lent & Easter Books 1 & 2
Celebrating Harvest
Celebrating Special Sundays

Anthologies of material for private reflection and public worship
A Word in Season
Liturgy of Life
Flowing Streams
Prayers for the Church Community

Cover design: Julian Smith
Cover photo: Sue Cunningham

Published by:
National Christian Education Council
Robert Denholm House
Nutfield
Redhill RH1 4HW

British Library Cataloguing-in-publication Data:
A catalogue record for this book is available
from the British Library.

ISBN 0-7197-0828-1

First published 1994
© 1994 Lesley Husselbee and Simon Oxley

All rights reserved. No part of this publication may be reproduced, stored
in a retrieval system, or transmitted in any form, electronic, mechanical,
photocopying, recording, or other means without the prior permission of
the publisher.

Typeset by Avonset, Midsomer Norton, nr. Bath
Printed in Great Britain by
Clifford Frost Ltd., Wimbledon, London

CONTENTS

FOREWORD TO THE SERIES

This is the final book in a series of six which offer services of worship for all ages in the church. The details of the other five can be found on the back cover of the book. The authors write from a wide experience of leading all-age worship and this series of books springs from that experience.

In the celebration of Christian worship every age-group has something to contribute. The experiences of each member of the congregation, regardless of age, can be used, and should be valued.

The ability and willingness of children to enter into a wide range of worship experiences should not be under-estimated. Adults should be encouraged to accept the gifts which children bring to worship. There is no 'audience' in all-age worship. The children are not performing for the adults; neither are they passive spectators to adult worship. These services provide the means by which the whole church family can engage in its most important responsibility and joy: the worship of God through Jesus Christ.

These books will serve churches best when a group of people, representative of all ages in the church meet to plan the worship, and are prepared to give time and thought to the preparation. Those who use them should feel free to adapt them to the needs of the local church community. In any one church they may well emerge on a Sunday morning looking quite different from the details given on the printed pages that follow.

Unless the flow of the service requires it no place is given for either the Lord's Prayer, the offertory, or announcements. These should be included according to local practice.

Donald Hilton
Series Editor

PREFACE

The Lord is risen!
He is risen indeed!

This ancient acclamation does not belong to Easter Day alone, although it finds great significance on that day when we celebrate the power of Jesus Christ over death and the grave. It is also a call to mission.

Indeed, it also belongs to Christmas and the vulnerable lordship we acknowledge in the Christ who came to live among his people, and began his lively progress from the manger, through the hills and plains of Galilee, to his victory through Calvary and the empty tomb.

This set of four services celebrates the Living Lord. The first service is designed for a Sunday close to Christmas and reminds us that we find the living Lord not only in the stable but amongst the poor and marginalized in our present society. The events in Bethlehem not only happened two thousand years ago; they are happening today.

The second service takes up the resurrection theme, but instead of turning to the resurrection stories at the end of the Gospel accounts, calls on the testimony of Paul and asks what it means to say that Jesus is alive.

The third service focuses on the mission of the Church through mission statements, stories and prayer whilst the final service rejoices in the universal Lord who is alive in all human relationships, in the breadth of the Church, and in the total span of creation. God has put all things under Christ's feet!

Lesley Husselbee
Simon Oxley

BETHLEHEM EVERYDAY
A Christmas service

Introduction
This service is designed to take place on a Sunday immediately before Christmas. Recognizing that the busyness of the season means that there is little time for learning words, a narrator tells the story. The service also acknowledges that the congregation will expect to hear - and see - the traditional Christmas story. However, it also seeks to help the congregation recognize that the birth of Jesus was not only an event which took place two thousand years ago, but that Christ is constantly being reborn into our human experience, and, as in Bethlehem, often among the least expected, the poor and the powerless. The service aims to express the tension in our understanding of Jesus as 'the one who came two thousand years ago' and 'the one who comes to every generation'.

Preparation
Appoint a narrator. S/he must speak clearly.
The Christmas story can be displayed in one of two ways:
Either plan a Christmas tableau with people taking the parts of Mary, Joseph, the shepherds, wise men and animals etc., and create an area in the church for the stable. Make animal-head shaped hats for people representing the animals to wear.
Or in advance of the service make models of Mary, Joseph etc. so that a crib scene can be set up at the front of the church as the service proceeds. Use plasticine or play-dough, or buy a commercial nativity frieze and use the cut-out figures. (*Bright Ideas, 'Christmas Art and Craft' from Scholastic Publications is a good resource for guidance on cribs and stars etc.*) Make a stable out of a large cardboard box and add some hay. This latter suggestion of a crib scene would be more effective in a smaller rather than a larger church, and would meet the problem of those churches with too few people to enlist for a tableau. In this latter case invite groups or families to make the star and little stars, sheep

and other animals, the stable scene, angels, kings and shepherds, Mary, Joseph, and the child in the manger. *(A Christmas Frieze, published by NCEC offers ideas for a cut out crib scene.)*

Whichever suggestion you follow try to arrange for a spotlight to illuminate the tableau/crib scene. It need be no more than one or two angle-poise lamps.

In a conspicuous place, set up a holder ready to receive four candles (in addition to the advent candles you may normally use) so that these can be lit and put in place during the prayers of intercession.

Select two speaking groups. Ideally there should be three or four people in each group, although if absolutely necessary one person could take the place of a group. The groups should rehearse their task and ensure that they speak clearly, and together. Group 1 will speak traditional words and should be dressed traditionally in suits or dresses. Their words are from the Authorised Version of the Bible. Group 2 will speak, almost as a chorus, contemporary words and should be dressed in more casual dress, e.g. jeans and sweater. The two groups should be seated on either side of the area where the tableau is to be created or the model crib scene set up. They remain there for the whole service.

ORDER OF SERVICE

As the organist or pianist finishes the normal musical voluntary, allow a brief moment of silence. In the silence light the appropriate advent candle, if this is your custom.

Choir, soloist or recorded music   'Away in the manger'
or other traditional hymn focussing on Jesus as a baby.

Call to worship
A child has been born to us, a son is given to us;
he will bear the symbol of dominion on his shoulder,
and his title will be:
Wonderful Counsellor, Mighty Hero,
Eternal Father, Prince of Peace.   *Isaiah 9.6 (REB)*

Hymn   'O little town of Bethlehem'

During the final verse of the hymn the two speaking groups step forward and take their places.

Prayer

Lord, your people long to see the one you have chosen! He is our counsellor and mighty hero. He is the prince of peace. Show us how to reach Bethlehem where he is born. Bring us running with the shepherds, and searching with the wise men. Let the star shine for us to guide us to the place where he lies in manger straw. Make Christmas real for us as we make our way to Bethlehem.

GROUP 1

Behold, I bring you good tidings of great joy, which shall be to all people. For unto you is born this day in the city of David a Saviour which is Christ the Lord.
Let us now go even unto Bethlehem, and see this thing which is come to pass, which the Lord has made known unto us.

Luke 2.10b-12, 15b (AV)

GROUP 2

Don't look for the baby Jesus
in the charming figures of the Christmas tableau.
Look for him among the homeless people of cardboard city.
Find him crouching in a shop doorway
covered by the remnants of yesterday's newspaper.
See him in the eyes of the beggar, hands outstretched,
and hear him in the silence of the children left at home alone as
parents celebrate elsewhere.

Narrator

In a small village called Nazareth lived a young woman named Mary. She was going to be married to Joseph, a carpenter. One day, before they were married, an angel came to Mary with a message from God. 'Don't be afraid, Mary,' he said. 'God has chosen you to be the mother of his Son. You are to call him Jesus.

The village of Nazareth where Mary and Joseph lived was in a country called Judea in the Roman Empire. One day, not long before Mary was due to have her baby, they heard that the Roman ruler had decided that he wanted to know exactly how many people were living in his lands. So he had passed a law making all the people in the empire go back to their place of birth to be counted. Joseph's family came from Bethlehem, so Mary and Joseph set off on their journey. It took several days.

Tableau: Those playing the part of Mary and Joseph walk around the church as though on a journey. They pause during the following hymn.
Crib scene: Those who have made the models of Mary and Joseph bring them to the front of the church.

Hymn 'In the bleak mid-winter'

Narrator
Tableau: As the narrator speaks Mary and Joseph act out his words, moving from imaginary inn to imaginary inn. As they approach the stable an innkeeper listens to their story and then shows them the stable. Light up the scene with a spotlight as they arrive.

When they arrived in Bethlehem they were very tired and could not find anywhere to stay because so many people had come to Bethlehem, and all the rooms were full. Joseph knew that Mary needed some rest. It was nearly time for the baby to be born. At last they came to another inn. The innkeeper had no rooms, but he offered them a place in a stable. They had to share with the animals but there was soft hay to lie on.

Crib scene: Those who have made animal models bring them to the front of the church, display the stable, and add the figures of Mary, Joseph and the animals. Light up the scene with a spotlight.

That night Mary's son was born. She wrapped Jesus up warmly and put him in the manger filled with hay.

Tableau: Mary places the baby in the manger.
Crib scene: Those who have made the models of manger and the child bring them to the front and place them in position.

GROUP 1

Behold, I bring you good tidings of great joy, which shall be to all people. For unto you is born this day in the city of David a Saviour which is Christ the Lord.
Let us now go even unto Bethlehem, and see this thing which is come to pass, which the Lord hath made known to us.

Hymn   'Once in royal David's City' *(First two verses only)*

Narrator
On the night that Jesus was born, some shepherds were out on the hills near Bethlehem, looking after their sheep. It was cold, and very dark. Suddenly the sky was filled with a bright and shining light. An angel from God came to tell them the good news that Jesus the Son of God was born. At first the shepherds were afraid, but the angel told them to go to Bethlehem to look for him.

GROUP 1

Let us now go even unto Bethlehem, and see this thing which is come to pass, which the Lord hath made known to us.

Hymn   'While shepherds watched their flocks' *(verses 1, 3, 4, 6)*

Narrator
They found Mary and Joseph, and the baby lying in a manger, just as the angel had said.

Tableau :The shepherds move around the church looking for the stable. When they find it they kneel before the child, and take their place in the tableau.
Crib scene: Those who have made the models of the shepherds and sheep place them in position.

GROUP 2

Don't look for the baby Jesus
in the charming figures of the Christmas tableau.
Look for him among the homeless people of cardboard city.
Find him crouching in a shop doorway
covered in the remnants of yesterday's newspaper.
See him in the eyes of the beggar, hands outstretched,
and hear him in the silence of the children left alone at home as
parents celebrate elsewhere.

Narrator

Meanwhile, some wise men who studied the stars, saw a very bright star in the sky. They believed it meant that a very special king was to be born. They enquired where such a king might be born. 'Bethlehem', they were told. They made haste to reach Bethlehem as soon as they could.

GROUP 1

Let us now go even unto Bethlehem, and see this thing which is come to pass, which the Lord hath made known to us.

Hymn   'As with gladness men of old' *(verses 1-3 only)*

Narrator

When the wise men found Jesus they presented him with gifts: gold, frankincense, and myrrh.

Tableau: The three wise men enter the church and, one by one present their gifts.
Crib scene: Those who have made models of the wise men place them in position.
As this happens the Group 2 readers speak their words, repeating them two or three times, or as long as it takes the wise men to enter, present their gifts, and take their places in the tableau.

GROUP 2

Don't look for the baby Jesus
in the charming figures of the Christmas tableau.
Look for him among the homeless people of cardboard city.
Find him crouching in a shop doorway
covered in the remnants of yesterday's newspaper.
See him in the eyes of the beggar, hands outstretched,
and hear him in the silence of the children left alone at home as
parents celebrate elsewhere.

Reading   John 1.1-4 and 10-14
Play quiet music (but not Christmas music) during this reading. Let the music continue for about one minute after the reading.

Reading *(read by one of the members of Group 2)*
Jesus was born in our world two thousand years ago
And yet,
And yet I know that he goes on being reborn.

It makes me think:
Where is Christ reborn today,
where I live?
Is he:
In the person next door;
the bag lady who begs outside the local church;
the single mother trying desperately to bring up her young child?
Is he reborn:
In the smartly dressed business-man;
the anoraked, trainer-clad child;
the white-haired lady who is the pillar of the church?
Is he reborn in me?
It makes you think!
If he's reborn in all of these people,
then it must make a difference to me.
It must mean that I am called to
serve them all in hope and joy, and to share the good news
with all I meet.

Today's visitors
The following people, leave their places in the congregation one by one and approach the tableau/crib. After saying their words they remain facing the manger, looking at the Christ child.

A typical British couple
If you were our baby, born here in *(mention your own town or village)* what would I hope for you? I hope you'd be clever and handsome, friendly and kind. You'd go to school in a smart, new uniform and perhaps come home, shoes scuffed, jumper torn. On to secondary school, then perhaps college or university. Yes, you'd have a good life here, my baby.
   Sleep safely here, little one.
An African woman *(preferably, a black member of the congregation or someone dressed for the part)*
If you were my baby and born in Africa, or another third world country, would you even reach the age of five to go to school?

You wouldn't have expensive toys and games, but would make them yourself out of bits of wood, tin or rubber. If you were lucky enough to be educated and travel, what would you think of the values in the Western world?

Sleep safely here, little one.

A man or woman dressed in old, worn clothes

If you were my baby and born in one of the many war-torn countries of the world, what sort of life would you have? You'd begin life with the sound of gunfire in your ears. With short supplies of food and limited medicine, with villages and towns being bombarded, there would be little chance of safety.

Sleep safely here, little one.

A single, British young woman

If you were my son and I your unmarried mother trying to feed you and keep you warm on social security what would you have? One small room with me and the danger of losing even that. The sneers of so many other people as you grew up with second-hand, ill-fitting clothes, and the constant fear that life would get worse rather than better.

Sleep safely here, little one.

adapted from an idea by Barbara Lambert

Hymn 'All poor men and humble'
    or 'Love came down at Christmas'

Prayers

Four people come from the congregation together bringing unlit candles. As they say their final sentence they place a candle in the prepared position and light it. Suggest to the congregation that they keep their eyes open during these prayers.

FIRST PERSON God of love, your Son, Jesus Christ, was born away from home and in the only place his desperate parents could find. We pray for all those who are homeless today:

    For those who live in the cardboard cities or shop doorways of our prosperous western towns,

    For those for whom inflation means that they cannot afford their mortgage and have lost their homes,

For those who have never known a true and loving home, and for all the agencies and organizations that seek to care for the homeless. At the manger of the child born away from home I light a candle for the homeless.

SECOND PERSON   God of love, your Son had to flee the country soon after his birth to escape death by King Herod. We pray for all refugees today:
> For those who have fled their homes because of war,
> For those who have left their countries for threat of torture,
> For those evicted by a policy of ethnic cleansing and racialism,
> For migrants driven from their homeland by starvation, and for all agencies that seek to help them.

At the manger of the refugee child, I light a candle for all refugees.

THIRD PERSON   God of love, your Son came to us as an ordinary human being, powerless, and with no special rights or privileges. We pray for the people of this world who are without power:
> For all children in danger of abuse,
> For women in societies dominated by men,
> For those persecuted for religious or political beliefs,
> and for all agencies that seek to empower them.

At the manger of the vulnerable child, I light a candle for the powerless.

FOURTH PERSON   God of love, you received visitors from distant lands at Bethlehem. We pray for the gift of peace:
> In places where racialism is openly manifest, or lies just beneath the surface,
> In lands where people are judged by the colour of their skin,
> In societies where there is a widening gap between rich and poor,

15

and for all people who seek harmony and
reconciliation.
At the manger of the Prince of Peace, I light a
candle for all people who are different from me.

As the prayers come to an end, the four people remain at the stable.

Groups 1 and 2 together
ALL   The Word became flesh; he made his home among us.
GROUP 1   First in Bethlehem,
GROUP 2   and now in every day, in every land, in every place, for
          every person.
GROUP 1   With shepherds and wise men;
GROUP 2   With undernourished children, the poor, and those who
          sleep covered with newspapers in doorways.

*Group 1 and Group 2 deliberately walk towards each other and mingle, to
form one group.*

ALL   A child has been born to us, a son is given to us;
          he will bear the symbol of dominion on his shoulder,
          and his title will be:
          Wonderful Counsellor, Mighty Hero,
          Eternal Father, Prince of Peace.

Isaiah 9.6 (REB)

Tableau: *All those who have formed the tableau move to seats scattered
throughout the congregation.*

Hymn   'O Come all ye Faithful'

Benediction

ALIVE!

A service to be used at Easter or to express the Church's Mission

Introduction

When Christians want to express their belief in the resurrection of Jesus they normally turn to the concluding chapters of the four Gospels. There they find, amongst other things, the story of the empty tomb, Jesus walking to Emmaus, and the disciples on the seashore. This service turns to Paul's letters rather than the Gospels, and takes as its basis Paul's argument for the resurrection. Since Paul was not a disciple of Jesus during his earthly life, and since he did not 'see Jesus' in resurrection like the other disciples he looks for Jesus' 'aliveness' and resurrection presence in other experiences. He did not go to the Easter morning garden, nor stand with Thomas, so he had to look into his own experience, and that of the Church of his time, for his evidence of resurrection.

Preparation

Choose five people to read the sections of 'It is the Lord'. Set up an overhead projector or flip chart. Find examples of inanimate and animate objects (*you will particularly need a stone, an effervescent tablet, a battery powered toy, a plant and a small caged animal*).

Search newspapers and religious magazines, and reflect on your own and other churches for 'signs of life' in the local and worldwide church. The magazines/journals of Christian Aid (or other Third World agencies) or missionary magazines will also be useful as a source of information. If such information is not already in story form, think how to express it in that way.

ORDER OF SERVICE

Call to Worship
Praised be the God and Father of our Lord Jesus Christ! In his
great mercy by the resurrection of Jesus from the dead, he gave
us new birth into a living hope.   *1 Peter 1.3(REB)*

Affirmation
*Plan for each section of the following to be read by a different person from
their place within the congregation.*
It is the Lord, in the dawning,
    in the renewal,
    in the arrival,
    in the new day.

It is the Lord, in the crowd,
    in the church,
    in the conversation,
    in the crisis.

It is the Lord, in our joys,
    in our sorrows,
    in our sickness,
    in our health.

It is the Lord, in the stable,
    in the humble,
    in the stranger,
    in the poor.

It is the Lord, risen and returned,
    alive for evermore,
    giving me new life,
    saving me in strife.

ALL   **It is the Lord.**

David Adam

Hymn   'Alleluia, alleluia give thanks to the risen Lord'

Prayer of Approach

Lord Jesus Christ,
to friend and enemy alike it must have seemed unbelievable.
They had seen you travel the road to Jerusalem,
and die on a a cross.
And now they said you were alive.
But for your friends who met you, the unbelievable came true.

Lord, now we look back through history to see your work on earth.
It seems unbelievable that you are alive.
But we meet you in friend and stranger,
in worship, and in the events of life
The unbelievable has come true for us.
You are alive,
And your living gives life to us.

Reading   Creed of Transformation

I believe in God
Who didn't create the world as something finished
as a thing which has to remain the same for ever
who doesn't rule by eternal laws which are irrevocable
nor by natural order of poor and rich
experts and uninformed
rulers and helpless.

I believe in God
who wants the conflict ended among the living
and the transformation of the existing
by our work
by our politics.

I believe in Jesus Christ
who was right when he
'an individual who cannot do anything'
like ourselves
worked on the transformation of all things in existence
and perished doing it.
Looking at him I realize
how our intelligence is crippled,

our fantasy suffocated,
our efforts wasted,
because we don't live the way he lived.
Every day I fear
that he died in vain
because he is buried in our churches
because we have betrayed his revolution
in obedience and fear
of the authorities.

I believe in Jesus Christ
Who rises into our lives
in order that we might be freed
from prejudice and arrogance
from fear and hatred
and may carry forward his revolution
towards his kingdom.

I believe in the spirit
who came with Jesus into the world,
in the community of all nations
and in our responsibility
for what will become of our earth,
a valley of misery, starvation and violence
or the city of God.
I believe in a just peace
which can be achieved
in the possibility of a meaningful life
for all people
in the future of this world of God.

Dorothy Soelle

Hymn   'Christ has risen while earth slumbers' *(available in Wild Goose Songs volume 2 'Enemy of Apathy')*

Leader
What is alive?

How can we tell whether something is alive or not? What conditions does anything have to fulfil to be called 'alive'? Let's experiment to find an answer, and look at various things to decide whether they are alive or not.

Show the following items and comment as necessary:
A stone
> It is totally inactive; clearly it is not alive.

An alka-seltzer or other effervescent tablet
> It looks like a stone at first, but what happens when it is put in water?

A battery powered toy
> It moves, acts, works, but is it alive?

A plant
> We know it lives, but it is static. How can we tell it is alive?

A pet mouse or hamster (in a cage, of course)
> Clearly it is very much alive. Is it more 'alive' than the plant?

A member of the congregation
> Does this person have to move to know s/he is alive?

What helps us know whether something is alive or not?
Invite members of the congregation to make suggestions and note them on an overhead projector or flip chart. Summarize the responses which might well include the following:
The evidence for life is that the object breathes . . . feeds . . . responds to its environment . . . grows and develops . . . reproduces etc.
Is that all that living is?
Is 'being alive' for us just the same as for a plant or a pet mouse. If there is more to living than that for human beings, then what is it that makes 'being alive' special for us as people?
Again, invite the members of the congregation to offer suggestions and note them on the overhead projector or flip chart. Their suggestions are likely to include:
> *The ability to reflect . . . to affect our environment . . . to create lasting relationships with others . . . to show compassion . . . to use the past and present to prepare for the future . . . to pray . . . to be aware of the spiritual dimension of life.*

For us these are just as important as criteria for 'being alive' as the biological signs of life such as breathing.

Hymn   'He is Lord, He is Lord'
             or 'For the beauty of the earth'

Reading   1 Corinthians 15.3-11

Bible study   *Jesus is alive*
Either silently or in buzz groups, invite the congregation to study the passage and to ask, 'How did Paul know that Jesus is alive?' As they think about the passage ask them to refer to the overhead projector/flip chart.

Ask how we can know today that Jesus is alive? Refer again to the overhead projector/flip chart. Comment on relationships, compassion, personal faith, spiritual experiences, the example of other believers, the growth of the church's life, an upsurge of goodness, signs of conversion, and the arrival of newcomers to the church etc.

Hymn   'Now the green blade riseth'

Stories   *Alive in the Church*
Share some stories about signs of life in the church. If possible use stories which are current in the religious press, and news from the local and worldwide church which have a particular relevance to the congregation. The following stories can also be used:

Inner city resurrection
The area was run down. Many people had moved away and whole areas of housing had been cleared. It looked as though the church might move away too.

The Anglican parish church, the Baptist church and the Methodist church all had building problems. Many members of their congregations travelled back to worship in an area where they had once lived. To many people it would have made sense to close down all three churches and encourage their members to worship closer to home.

That's probably what would have happened if a few people had not believed that God still had work for the church to do in the area. They had a struggle to convince other people that it was both right and possible. Quite remarkably the money was found to build a shared church. Anglicans, Baptists and Methodists had to discover how they could worship and work together.

It wasn't an easy process and life together in the new church building has been made difficult by constant vandalism. But new members have joined from the local area and the church continues to witness to the living Christ in the area.

Taken from the experience of Harpurhey United Church, Manchester.

Resurrection through community

It isn't only church buildings which can bring hope to an area. In the state of Andhra Pradesh in Southern India, a group of Indian Christians work to give people the chance of life. One project in which they have been involved, helped by Christians in other parts of the world, is building community halls in remote villages. You can't get to these villages by car or even by bullock cart. The road turns into a track and then into a footpath. To encourage completion of the buildings, the villagers are expected to build the walls and the project supplies the roofing materials.

How do these simple buildings offer hope? They give a place for the villagers to meet so they can decide how to run village life. They give a place for classes to help people learn to read and write. They give a place for people to store their crops - otherwise they have to sell them straight away to people who can store them. If they store them and sell later, the villagers get a better price.

The group is also building a conference centre to help their members follow Jesus. The centre will also be a farm which will show people how to grow crops and look after farm animals.

The new life the members have found in Jesus Christ is giving other people the possibility of life.

Tell other stories as they are available to you such as the revival of faith in someone who had left the church for several years, or of marriage renewal after difficulties. Remind people of the way in which some of the hostages in Beirut emerged as stronger people, experiencing a resurrection from the gloom of their imprisonment.

Leader   *Alive in us (based on 1 Corinthians 12.27)*
Is the body of Christ in this place alive?
Remind the congregation about what has been said about being alive by referring again to the overhead projector/flip chart.
Is this local church alive by these criteria?
Paul was convinced that Christ is alive through his own story and the story of others. Do people encounter the living Christ when they encounter the body of Christ, the church?

Prayers of Confession and Intercession

Father, you give life with absolute generosity.
We confess to you that too often
> our actions and our attitudes deny life to others;
> our worship ceases to be lively;
> our faith has become lifeless.

Father, by the power of your love you raised Jesus.
Bring new life to our living and our worship as you forgive us.
We pray for those:
Whose lives are threatened because they have been denied food and drink and medication, remembering especially . . .
Whose lives are confined by their circumstances, physical disability or prison cell, remembering especially . . .
Whose enjoyment of a full life has been destroyed through broken relationships, lost jobs and homelessness, remembering especially. . .
Who work to bring life through giving aid, reconciling, healing and sharing the good news of a living Lord, remembering especially . . .
We offer our prayers through Jesus Christ who in his living, dying and rising showed us life and offered life to all.

Ideally, move into a celebration of the Lord's Supper. Whether or not they receive the bread and wine, children should remain in the congregation. If Communion is not to be included in the service, end with the final hymn. A full order for the Lord's Supper is not given; plan the service according to your own custom. The following thanksgiving prayer can be used.

Prayer of thanksgiving

To the words: for every sign of life, for every sign of love, invite the response:
Thanks be to God.

> You are the creator of all that is.
> You give life to every creature.
> For every sign of life, for every sign of love:
>> **Thanks be to God**
> You have given life to us, and given us the power to enjoy it.
> For every sign of life, for every sign of love:
>> **Thanks be to God**

You have not abandoned us
even when we have denied your life within us.
For every sign of life, for every sign of love:
> **Thanks be to God**

Your love has been made human in Jesus
and he shared our life.
For every sign of life, for every sign of love:
> **Thanks be to God**

His words, actions and his whole person
were filled with your life for us.
For every sign of life, for every sign of love:
> **Thanks be to God**

We tried to end that life on a cross: but even death cannot kill life.
For every sign of life, for every sign of love:
> **Thanks be to God**

The living Lord met his friends on the day of resurrection
and meets us here today.
For every sign of life, for every sign of love:
> **Thanks be to God**

The Spirit stirs us up and equips us
so that we can be your lively people.
For every sign of life, for every sign of love:
> **Thanks be to God**

You prepare a table for us
and the bread and wine are signs for us of your life.
For every sign of life, for every sign of love:
> **Thanks be to God**

Now come to live in us that we may live in you.

Hymn   'Christ is alive! Let Christians sing'
            or 'Let us talents and tongues employ'

Benediction

GO INTO ALL THE WORLD

Introduction

This service aims to help the congregation to share their faith with other people, and by learning more about the needs of the neighbourhood, decide how to put their faith into action. It involves thinking about the potential for mission in their own area. By redefining mission in a new statement, and offering examples by stories, it encourages each member of the congregation to re-value the mission in which they are already involved and to be challenged to new mission tasks in proclamation and service.

Preparation

Prepare a large map of the area which the church serves. This could be a commercial map or a simple outline, drawn with felt-tip pen, on a large piece of paper. Indicate some obvious landmarks, and add local facilities such as old people's homes, day centres, sheltered housing, half-way houses for prisoners, or homes for handicapped people etc.

Cut 'people-shapes' from coloured paper and attach small pieces of Blu-tak to the back of them, ready to stick them onto the map during the service.

Have ready a large piece of paper, flip chart, or overhead projector. This will be used to write up ideas suggested by the congregation.

ORDER OF SERVICE

Call to Worship

Go therefore to all nations and make them my disciples; baptize them in the name of the Father and the Son and the Holy Spirit, and teach them to observe all that I have commanded you. I will be with you always, to the end of time. *Matthew 28.19-20 (REB)*

Hymn   'Christ is the King! O Friends rejoice'
              'Sing, one and all, a song of celebration'
              or any other hymn expressing praise, and a sense of call.

Prayer
Every day,
living God,
every day we will wake
to speak of you;
not in choice language
and perfect paragraphs
> but in the way we expect your surprises,
> in the delight we take in sharing your healing moments,
> in the determination you give us
>> to be a refuge for the battered and the bruised,
>> a rock for the tossed and troubled,
>> and a harbour for the grieving and angry.

Every day,
we will seek to be a witness for you,
> not through articulate testimony
> or a vast wardrobe of texts
but through the brightness of our faces
> when pain is all we feel inside,
and through the hope our eyes disclose
> as we share another's sadness.

Every day,
we will proclaim the miracle of your love
not limited by narrow horizons of church, nation and self
but by breathing the pure, open air of your Spirit
> by which the light of nations can shine
> and all be reconciled to you in Jesus Christ.

Every day,
we will rejoice and be glad for all
who, knowing you as loving Lord,
draw the world's attention
not to themselves
but to Jesus Christ
who alone deserves the glory for ever and ever. Amen

David Jenkins (adapted)

Discovering the local area

If possible send a few people of mixed ages out of the church and ask them to walk around the immediate area. They should try to look at the surroundings as though for the first time and discover the church's task in mission and care, in the area. They should be ready to be interviewed on return.

Whilst they are out, invite each member of the congregation to write down the principal buildings they recall from the area in the vicinity of the church. Display a large map of the area and indicate the buildings mentioned. What do these buildings suggest the mission and ministry of the church should be? Write these ideas on an overhead projector/flip chart.

Alternatively, invite a local councillor or other person who knows the area well to suggest what role the church might play in the community.

When those who have walked around the area return, interview them to discover if they have seen anything that has given new insights into the needs of the area and the tasks of the church.

Prayer

Invite the congregation to reflect silently on the needs of the local area, and to turn these thoughts into silent prayers. Conclude with the following:

Accept our prayers, Lord.
Help us to remember that you came
and lived and died
so that all those who believe in you
may have life in all its fullness.
Thanks be to God. Amen

Hymn   'Colours of the day dawn into the mind'
or 'Come let us remember the joys of the town'

Reading   Matthew 28.16-20

Mission redefined (*Use several voices to read the following*)
Mission advertises God's love. It takes place under God's initiative, and finds its mainspring in the insights and message of the Bible.

Mission is the announcement which takes into account all we have experienced in Jesus.

Mission marks the rejection of all that separates, injures, and destroys, recognizing that ultimately these things have been overcome by what unites and heals and creates.

Mission calls individuals and groups to witness to God who, furthering his purpose, encourages, calls in question, changes, condemns, and gives greater awareness, within all aspects of human experience.

Mission leads to personal and corporate growth as we reach towards the maturity we see in Jesus, and thus creates an openness to the perceptions of other Christians.

Mission involves a willingness to listen to, and be changed by, those to whom mission is directed.

Mission involves a commitment to working for a just and human society in every area of life, and in all the structures of society.

Mission respects the integrity of God's creation.

Mission is a call to people to commit themselves to Jesus Christ, and to share with his people in the life of the Church.

A Norfolk theological working party

Hymn   'God's Spirit is in my heart'

Mission stories *The following two stories are based on actual people, though the names and some circumstances have been changed.*

Sarah
Sarah was feeling very depressed. She ought not to have done. She had a loving husband and family, and they had just had a new baby - a baby they had wanted for a long time. But somehow things weren't quite as they had expected. Baby Clyde seemed to cry all the time, especially at night; and Sarah always felt tired. Her husband George worked long hours; he had to keep up with the mortgage. If grandparents had lived nearby it would have been different, but they didn't; they lived miles away. Frankly too, Sarah missed the responsible job she was doing before Clyde was born.

She got talking to Christine in the supermarket. She hadn't really known her before, but she had a smiling face and a sympathetic smile. She seemed to understand. They met at the shops, then visited each other for coffee, then later for a meal. 'Come round to the Parents and Toddlers Club I go to', Christine said. It met in the local church hall. It was an eye-opener for Sarah. She discovered just how many other mothers felt the same emotions and anxieties she felt.

Sarah was never quite sure when she first discovered that Christine went to church - the same church where the Parents and Toddler's Club was held. Neither could she ever remember when she decided to try it out for herself. Perhaps it was that special service they had for Parents and their babies? Or was it just that Christine suggested it and she agreed? Anyway, go she did, and she found she liked it. Her - Sarah who had never set foot in a church for ages apart from the occasional family wedding! George tried it too, hesitantly at first, but then with more confidence, especially when he saw that two of his mates from the factory also went.

There were no flashing lights from heaven. No dramatic conversion. It just felt good and right to be there and to share the fellowship. It was only last week they asked her if she would join the choir. Well, why not? They said at school she had a better voice than most. She'd think about it, she said. Yes, of course, she'd think about it . . .

David

David was at his wits end. He was a singer with a pop group and had always hoped he might one day see his name in the bright lights of the West End. But he had made the mistakes that everyone had warned him about and which he thought he could avoid. Alcohol, first; too much of it and too often. Then drugs. 'Try it', someone had said. 'It will give you confidence when you go on stage. You can always give it up when you no longer need it'. But he found he always did need it, more and more, and his work began to suffer. The group broke up and no-one else would take him on. Months of being out of work followed.

At his depths of depression he was invited to a party. He'd been told that drugs would be freely available. Arriving early he was shown into the living room. 'Under the coffee table', someone told him, 'there's plenty there'. As he reached the coffee table he saw a colourful booklet lying on the top. 'Good News for Modern Man' was the title. 'I'm a modern man,' David said to himself, 'and I sure need some good news at this moment.' He picked the book up and put it into his pocket to read later.

Back home he opened the booklet - and threw it on the floor in disappointment and disgust. It was a modern version of Mark's Gospel. How it had found its way to the coffee table of that house remains a mystery. It was three days later before he bothered to pick it up. Idly he began to read it. Slowly he became engrossed. It was over an hour later before he put it down. 'This man,' he read, as he approached the end of the Gospel, 'was really the Son of God.' The words entered his life. He was a changed man.

No-one should doubt the agony and indecision that followed and the pain of re-adjusting his life-style. But the change had been made and the barrier crossed as he confessed Christ as his Lord.

Tell other local stories of how people came to faith or how they felt called to serve people in Christ's name. This might be done at a gentle level by inviting one or two people in advance of the service to tell how they first started coming to church. Select both people who have been in the church a long time and others more recently arrived. Try to represent several age-groups. If people are shy suggest they be interviewed.

Hymn   'Amazing grace (how sweet the sound)'
or 'Moses, I know you're the man'

Mission involvement
Remind people of the 'Mission redefined' statement, and invite as many as will to move to the front of the church, pick up a 'people shape', and stick it on the building or area in which they believe they are already involved in mission and service. Shops, schools, social service department, homes, for example, may be so identified. Suggest that in fact everyone in the church could have come to the front because we are all involved in the mission of the church in our own way.

Meditation
Photocopy the following meditation for the whole congregation and invite them to read it as a silent prayer. Alternatively, the leader should read it aloud. Note that there is no copyright problem for this item.

God has created me to do him some definite service. He has committed some work to me which he has not committed to another. I have my mission . . .

31

I am a link in the chain, a bond of connection between persons.
He has not created me for naught.
I shall do good. I shall do his work. I shall be an angel of peace, a
preacher of truth in my own place, even while not intending it, if
I do but keep his commandments.
Therefore I will trust him. Wherever, whatever I am, I can never
be thrown away. If I am in sickness, my sickness may serve him;
in perplexity, my perplexity may serve him; if I am in sorrow, my
sorrow may serve him . . .
He knows what he is about.

John Henry Newman (abridged)

*Follow the meditation with the following prayer. After each section of the
prayer invite the congregation to respond with a simple sung prayer-verse
such as:*
'Kindle a flame to lighten the dark'
or 'O Lord, hear my prayer'
or 'Ubi Caritas'

Prayer

Lord Jesus Christ, you gave special care to the disabled and those
damaged by life's misfortunes. We bring before you in love those in
our own society whose lives are made more difficult by accident or
difficulty.

Prayer verse to be sung by the congregation

Lord Jesus Christ, sick people never came to you in vain. Many were
healed and all felt themselves encircled by your love. We bring before
you those in our society who are in hospital, detained at home
through illness, or facing an operation.

Prayer verse to be sung by the congregation

Lord Jesus Christ, you yourself knew what it was to wander the
country with no secure place of rest, no roof above your head to
shelter you. We bring before you those in our society who are
homeless, those living rough on the streets, sheltered only by a
cardboard box.

Prayer verse to be sung by the congregation

Lord Jesus Christ, you were yourself a refugee and you showed care
for foreigners and those pushed into the margins of life. We bring

before you the political refugees of our time, victims of racial violence in our own society, and all victimized because of their place of birth or colour of skin.
Prayer verse to be sung by the congregation

Lord Jesus Christ, once you were alone in the distress of Gethsemane, left isolated on the cross. We bring to you those in our society who are lost in loneliness. We pray for young mothers who feel trapped in their homes, the elderly imprisoned by infirmity, and all who dare not face the danger of night-time streets.
Prayer verse to be sung by the congregation

Lord Jesus Christ, you came to call people to a living relationship with God. We bring to you those whose lives seem pointless, those at the end of their tether, those searching for a spiritual significance they cannot find without finding you.
Prayer verse to be sung by the congregation

Take our lives, Lord, we dedicate them to you.
Give us eyes to see the needs of others,
ears to hear the cry of those in need,
and sensitivity to know when to speak the word of challenge.
We will be your hands and feet,
your voice and your presence
and as you gave yourself to us
we will give ourselves to you through others.

Hymn   'Lord, you give the great commission'
               or 'O Jesus, I have promised'

Benediction
Send us out
in the power of your Spirit
to live and work
to your praise and glory. Amen

33

MAKING CONNECTIONS
Celebrating the universal Christ

Introduction
We often limit human relationships - and even our salvation in Christ - to the narrow area of our own personal and church experience. This service is designed to give a visual image of the Christian belief that all life is inter-connected, and ultimately held in unity by Christ. He is 'the supreme Lord over all things.'

Preparation
Prepare placards of a suitable size to be held by members of the congregation and which can be read by everyone in church. For the words on each placard, see the Order of Service.

Obtain an adequate supply of wool depending upon the size of the congregation and how it is spread out in the church. The wool can be made up of odd balls left over from knitting. Balls of string could also be used.

Invite one person to be the 'focus person', and two more to be 'connectors', see details in the Order of Service. In advance of the service the focus person should be sitting in the middle of the congregation.

ORDER OF SERVICE

Call to Worship
God put all things under Christ's feet and gave him to the church as supreme Lord over all things.

Ephesians 1.22 (GNB)

Prayer of Approach
You are Lord of all things:
everything we can see, touch, hear, smell and taste;
everything we know, and things beyond our imagination.

You are Lord of the church:
>   this church gathered together for worship,
>   the other churches in our town,
>   churches in every part of the world.

You are Lord of our lives:
>   each one of us,
>   all people.

We come to worship you - our Lord, Lord of the Church, and Lord of all things. Help us in our worship to celebrate our relationship with you, with each other and with your world. Amen

Hymn   'Think of a world without any flowers'
>   *or* 'Lord of the boundless curves of space'

Responsive Psalm

LEADER   Give thanks to the Lord because he is good;
RESPONSE   **His love lasts for ever**.
LEADER   By his wisdom he made the heavens and the earth;
RESPONSE   **His love lasts for ever.**
LEADER   He made the sun and the moon, day and night;
RESPONSE   **His love lasts for ever.**
LEADER   When his people were in slavery, he set them free;
RESPONSE   **His love lasts for ever.**
LEADER   He promises us a kingdom where his will is done;
RESPONSE   **His love lasts for ever**
LEADER   He provides food for every living creature;
RESPONSE   **His love lasts for ever.**
LEADER   Give thanks to the God of heaven;
RESPONSE   **His love lasts for ever.**

Adapted from Psalm 136

Interconnected

Ask the 'focus person' who represents everyone present in worship to stand in the middle of the area where the congregation is sitting, and the two 'connectors' to be ready.

Hand out at random throughout the congregation placards bearing words as indicated below:

> *the name of your church*
> *your denomination*
> *your world-denominational affiliation (e.g. Anglican Communion, Reformed Church, World Council of Churches)*

the name of your town	*county*	*nation*
family	*neighbours*	*place of work*
place of leisure	*charities*	*local shops*
European countries	*World countries*	

Add any local or topical interests as names on the placards and keep a few placards available for additional names that emerge during the service.

Give the two 'connectors' balls of different coloured wool. Ask members of the congregation to suggest where there are obvious connections between the organizations or groups on the placards. For example, there will be a connection between the 'focus person', the local church, the denomination, and the world body. The 'connector' should make the connections visible by running a length of wool between the various people holding the placards.

Continue the exercise. Some people will be linked to charities as workers or givers. There will be links with local shops. Some will have friends in other countries. Two people may play golf and so be connected, or belong to the same leisure group.

Don't rush this exercise. It is more than an introductory activity. It aims to help the members of the congregation to think about the inter-connectedness of their lives. It should quickly become an almost impossible exercise as more and more people find links with each other, and the end result should be a widespread web of connections. As the exercise continues invite the congregation to reflect on the meaning of the connections.

Collect up the lengths of wool and place them on one side for later use.

Prayer of Thanksgiving and Confession

Lord, we have seen how we are linked together with other people throughout the world. We thank you for our relationships with our family, our neighbours and our friends in this church. We thank you for the way we depend for our life and our faith on people we do not, and may never, meet but who are vital to us.

Add other appropriate thanksgiving for the life of the church and arising from the activity.

We confess that we have used our relationship and connections for our own advantage. We have taken without giving. We take the raw materials of faith and food from those near us and those who live far away.

We want what others can give to us but we don't want to give to them. Father forgive us and help us to rejoice in the rich web of connections which shape our living.

Hymn   'Song of Caedmon'
                or 'Almighty Father of all things that be'

Leader
In our worship we have praised God as creator and we have seen how we are all linked together in life, but we best understand God through his Son, Jesus Christ. We claim that he is central to all we are and do. Where do we see Jesus in our picture of connections? Perhaps there is more than one answer to this vital question.

For example, he is a part of our human connections.
Call one person out of the congregation. Place them apart from everyone else. Give them a placard bearing the name 'Jesus'. Invite the congregation to suggest how the 'focus person', who represents everyone in the congregation may be connected with Jesus. Of course, by the grace of God, there is always the potential for a direct link between every person and Jesus but, in fact, most of us found an initial connection through friends, the local church, a church organization etc. You may even need to write new placards to meet the experience of some member of the congregation, for example, some are first connected to Jesus through reading the Bible. With wool of a single colour, make the connections between Jesus, the 'focus person' and all relevant placards.

Collect up the lengths of wool and place them at the back of the church.

Leader
But there are other answers to our question? Our next hymn may give us a clue.

Hymn   'Jesus shall reign where'er the sun'
                or 'God's glory fills the universe'
                or 'Thou art the everlasting Word'

Move the person with the Jesus placard into the heart of the congregation. As you do so invite suggestions about how Jesus links with each of the other organizations or groups represented by the placards. Express these by linking Jesus in a second coloured wool to all other people holding placards, as the point is made.

37

*Quickly produce two more placards '**Past**' and '**Future**'. How does Jesus connect with these? As the answers emerge, add the connections.*
Collect up the lengths of wool and place them at the back of the church.

Bible Study Read Colossians 1.15-20.
Create buzz groups (three or four people talking to each other wherever they may be sitting) or invite a pre-arranged group to sit at the front and study the passage so that everyone else can hear what they say.

Leader
What is the role of Christ in the universe according to this reading? It suggests a very different picture. More than human relations are expressed. In the beginning and in the end, it is God in Christ who unites all things.
*Take further wool and extend it from the '**Jesus**' placard to as near the four corners of the church as possible. Then collect up the lengths of wool and place them at the back of the church.*

Te Deum Today
Let us respond in praise using a modern version of an old Christian hymn.

God, with every breath, we join in the ovation to you
the greatest; we cheer shout and applaud you.

Universes beyond sight and sound dance to your tune:
composer, arranger, performer; without equal before or since.

Forces beyond intellect, insight and imagination chorus
in harmony with mysterious voices deep down and within.

God, you perform solo, spotlit and gracefully:
applauding stars blaze with reflected radiance,
all who bring their friends, cheer,
those who sacrifice most, cheer,
even all the critics, cheer.

East and west, north and south, audiences shout and stamp,
clapping loudly as you move everyone to sing
and shower their bouquets
on the only one who imitates you to perfection.

38

Christ, today you are in the limelight
Son of God for ever and ever.

Your humanity gives us liberty:
our birth is honoured by your beginning
and our death by your discordant end
when you bring to their feet all who stay for the final act.

Though now you are with God in splendour,
we are together, our lives reviewed by yours.

Through your blood given freely
transfuse us with new life;

that we may remain with you
and with all who have gone before
to share your perpetual, timeless joy.

Tony Burnham

Offering
In addition to the normal offering of money add the wool from the various activities as a symbol of the total inter-connectedness of all people, groups and the universe itself.
> Lord, we bring this money,
> all the connections that link our lives together,
> and ourselves.
> Use everything we offer in the work of your kingdom.

Hymn   'Brother, sister, let me serve you'
              or 'As the bride is to her chosen'

Prayers of Intercession
Use a sung response such as:
'Through our lives and by our prayers, your kingdom come.'
> Sometimes we think we don't need other people.
> We can make our own life and our own faith.
> As we remember the ways in which we are linked to each other
> and to God,
> let us pray for those to whom our lives are linked.
> **Through our lives and by our prayers, your kingdom come.**

Let us pray for those who are closest to us - our family and friends,
the people we work with and play with,
The people who live in our street; especially . . .
Through our lives and by our prayers, your kingdom come.

Let us pray for our church, the churches of our town, of our denomination and the world family of God's people;
for a sharing of resources and experience;
for openness to one another and to the Holy Spirit; especially . . .
Through our lives and by our prayers, your kingdom come.

Let us pray for all those to whom our lives are linked in this town,
this country and the world;
for those who suffer from the lack of the basics of life
    because we have taken more than we need;
for those who work to bring justice into international relations and world trades; especially . . .
Through our lives and by our prayers, your kingdom come.

Let us pray for ourselves that we may rejoice in the rich variety of
    relationships that God has given us; especially . . .
Through our lives and by our prayers, your kingdom come.

Hymn   'We turn to you, O God of every nation'

Benediction

ACKNOWLEDGMENTS

The editor and publisher gratefully acknowledge permission to reproduce the following copyright material.

Every effort has been made to trace copyright owners but if any rights have been inadvertently overlooked, the necessary correction will be made in subsequent editions. We apologise for any apparent negligence.

David Adam:
> *Tides and Seasons* © Triangle/SPCK 1989 as quoted in *Bread for Tomorrow* SPCK/Christian Aid, used by permission

Tony Burnham:
> *Te deum Today* used by permission

David Jenkins:
> *Every day Living God* used by permission

Barbara Lambert:
> *Today's visitors* adapted and reprinted by permission

Dorothy Soelle:
> *Creed of Transformation*

A Norfolk theological working party:
> *Mission redefined* reprinted by permission

We are grateful for permission to quote from the following versions of the Bible:

REB   The Revised English Bible (© 1989 Oxford and Cambridge University Presses).

AV   Authorized Version.

GNB   Good News Bible (The Bible Societies/Collins Publishers) - Old Testament © American Bible Society 1976; New Testament © American Bible Society 1966, 1971, 1976.

A Collection Of Collections

LITURGY OF LIFE

Compiled by Donald Hilton.

In corporate acts of worship in all the mainstream churches the same basic elements can be seen. This anthology broadly follows the liturgy of the Churches bringing into the sanctuary the everyday experiences and thoughts which interlock with the main components of Christian worship.

Liturgy of Life is intended both to aid personal devotion and reflection, and also to provide material for Christian education and worship.

FLOWING STREAMS

Compiled by Donald Hilton.

Countless streams of human experiences flow through the Bible narratives and the same emotions flow through human life in our time. In this anthology these contemporary experiences mingle, page by page, with the experiences recorded in the Bible. Everyday life thus becomes a comment on the Bible stories, and the biblical events help to interpret our life today.

TURN BUT A STONE

By Edmund Banyard

This new collection of prayers and meditations written by Edmund Banyard is intended as a stimulation to thought, both for personal devotion and as an aid in corporate worship. It expands on the themes of the Bible readings suggested in the *Joint Liturgical Group Lectionary (JLG2)*.

Edmund's earlier book *Word Alive*, an anthology of works from around the world, was used as a companion to the previous lectionary (JLG1).

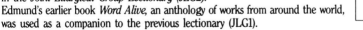

REFLECTIONS

By Cyril Franks.

The Gospels speak to us today and every day. In this collection of thirty-one readings from St Matthew's Gospel we are invited to draw nearer to Christ as we reflect on Matthew's writings in our daily lives. Each passage is accompanied by a thought-provoking meditation.

A WEALTH OF WORSHIP AND LEARNING RESOURCES FROM NCEC

Available from your local Christian bookshop or, in case of difficulty, from NCEC direct.

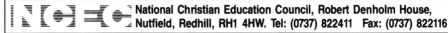

National Christian Education Council, Robert Denholm House, Nutfield, Redhill, RH1 4HW. Tel: (0737) 822411 Fax: (0737) 822116

MORE RESOURCES FOR ALL AGE WORSHIP FROM NCEC

CELEBRATING SERIES

Compiled by
Donald Hilton

CHRISTMAS BOOKS 1 & 2

LENT & EASTER BOOKS 1 & 2

HARVEST

SPECIAL SUNDAYS

FESTIVAL SERVICES for the Church Year

Sold individually or in a set with a substantial saving

Available from all good Christian bookshops or, in case of difficulty, from NCEC direct.

Other Titles from RADIUS and NCEC

THE HILL
Sylvia Read
0-7197-0761-7

A modern mystery play in which the characters find themselves caught up in the experience of Easter. 30 mins.

Code No. PLA0761 (A)

CROSSTALK
Bob Irving
0-7197-0795-1

A collection of ten short plays based upon the parables which were, in their own time, sharp contemporary stories in an established tradition. In order to convey the same sense of immediacy these sketches are presented in a highly modern quick-firing style. No need for props or costumes, maximum cast of five. Each play lasts about 5 minutes.

Code No. PLA0795 (A)

SURPRISE SKETCHES
Ronald Rich
0-7197-0796-X

Five one-act plays with surprising endings. Ideal as a prompter for discussion or for use in worship, these plays examine some familiar human failings in a new stimulating style. Each play runs for about 10 minutes.

Code No. PLA0796 (A)

THE FLAME
Edmund Banyard
0-7197-0709-9

A novel approach to the idea of Pentecost, this play is a one act fantasy in the style of the Theatre of the Absurd. Four ordinary people are offered the 'Light of the World' by a messenger from the border between Time and Eternity. 25 mins.

Code No. FLA0709 (A)

> Performance times given are
> very approximate.

A FISTFUL OF FIVERS
Edmund Banyard
0-7197-0667-X

Twelve five-minute plays, each with a Christian message. Using the minimum of actors, scenery and props, these lively sketches will appeal to everyone who is young in the widest sense.

Code No. PLA0667 (A)

A FUNNY THING HAPPENED ON THE WAY TO JERICHO
Tom Long
0-7197-0722-6

The dress rehearsal for a presentation of the Good Samaritan turns out to be more than the leading player intended, as she is challenged by each of the roles she takes on in her search for the one she feels happy with. 30 mins.

Code No. FUN0722 (A) R

THE PRODIGAL DAUGHTER
William Fry
0-7197-0668-8

Using a neat twist, William Fry has turned one of the best-known parables into the tale of a present-day girl, updating the setting to portray some of the concerns of modern society. While it shows the seamier side of contemporary life, the message of this play is ultimately one of redemption and love. 30 mins.

Code No. PLA0668 (A)

NATIVITY LETTERS
Nick Warburton
0-7197-0724-2

Highlights the strains put on mother and daughter in the interdependence of a single parent family, which make them tend to disassociate themselves from other people. Help eventually presents itself through a committed teacher in the daughter's drama group. 40 mins.

Code No. NAT0724 (A)

WHO'LL BE BROTHER DONKEY?
Arthur Scholey
0-7197-0723-4

Three traditional Christmas tales are combined to produce this play where the animals use their Christmas Eve gift of speech to enact the crib scene in the hillside chapel. During the journey from their stable they outwit the wily Fox and Vixen in their malevolent schemes. The conclusion shows how the preparation of the crib scene is achieved against all odds through forgiveness of their fellow creatures and faith. 60 mins.

Code No. WHO0723 (A)